YOUR KNOWLEDGE HAS VALUE

- We will publish your bachelor's and master's thesis, essays and papers

- Your own eBook and book - sold worldwide in all relevant shops

- Earn money with each sale

Upload your text at www.GRIN.com
and publish for free

Bibliographic information published by the German National Library:

The German National Library lists this publication in the National Bibliography; detailed bibliographic data are available on the Internet at http://dnb.dnb.de .

This book is copyright material and must not be copied, reproduced, transferred, distributed, leased, licensed or publicly performed or used in any way except as specifically permitted in writing by the publishers, as allowed under the terms and conditions under which it was purchased or as strictly permitted by applicable copyright law. Any unauthorized distribution or use of this text may be a direct infringement of the author s and publisher s rights and those responsible may be liable in law accordingly.

Imprint:

Copyright © 2015 GRIN Verlag, Open Publishing GmbH
Print and binding: Books on Demand GmbH, Norderstedt Germany
ISBN: 9783668265387

This book at GRIN:

http://www.grin.com/en/e-book/335519/is-the-world-less-violent-in-modern-times

Mohammad Ahmed Hotiana

Is the world less violent in modern times?

Implications of science and global politics on world peace

GRIN Publishing

GRIN - Your knowledge has value

Since its foundation in 1998, GRIN has specialized in publishing academic texts by students, college teachers and other academics as e-book and printed book. The website www.grin.com is an ideal platform for presenting term papers, final papers, scientific essays, dissertations and specialist books.

Visit us on the internet:

http://www.grin.com/

http://www.facebook.com/grincom

http://www.twitter.com/grin_com

Is the world less violent in modern times?

Implications of science, global politics etc. on world peace

Author:

Mohammad Ahmed Hotiana

Forman Christian College (A Chartered University)

IS THE WORLD LESS VIOLENT IN MODERN TIMES?

Abstract:

Events such as great breakthroughs in science, change in political infrastructures, spread of knowledge and education, creation of high-tech weaponry, religious terrorism, and war on terror .etc. have greatly affected societies, nations and the wider world. This has made everyone; from a layman to a military personnel and from a diplomat to a scientist, question if these changes in the world around us have contributed in making the world a less violent place or otherwise.

Due to a variety of different opinions and ideas; scholars, institutions, governments and other organizations are working towards finding solutions to this question. However, the global community has not yet been able to achieve consciences on the answer to this question. Furthermore, I believe that due to difference in ideologies, interests and conditions it would be impossible to find an answer that is acceptable to or agreed upon by all.

In this research paper, we shall try to discuss if the modern times are less violent or is it the other way around. To do so, we would be using some arguments by John Avery, as portrayed in his writing: **Space age science and stone-age politics,** in order to discuss how modern science and technology have produced evils that contribute to global violence. In addition, we would use his work to assess some factors in the world of today that neglect the hypothesis that the world of today is a less violent place.

Furthermore, we would rely on: **The better angels of our nature** by Steven Pinker to find arguments suggesting that violence has been in decline for a while now. In addition, we would try to examine his idea of the world being at the most peaceful stage in the history of the human race.

IS THE WORLD LESS VIOLENT IN MODERN TIMES?

We would be using some statistical data and other resources in order to find answers to the following questions:

1. Does modern science play a role in peace making or does it work against it?
2. Do nationalism and the creation of states help in making the world less violent?
3. Does abolition of punishments like death penalty decrease violence?
4. What is the contribution of education and economics towards a world with less violence?
5. How effective is the role of international peace-making systems?

Answering these questions would help us get a clearer image of the aspects that affect the violence and hence would help us find the answer to the initial question: Is the world less violent in modern times?

IS THE WORLD LESS VIOLENT IN MODERN TIMES?

Does modern science play a role in peace making or does it work against it?

Modern science has greatly contributed in providing individuals and societies with a life of comfort and luxury. In addition, aspects like improved transportation, communication, health care facilities .etc. owe their existence to science.

However, there is another side to the story that cannot be neglected. It is that science has also provided humans with the technology that could be used to bring an end to our civilization. Such technologies include; armory, weapons of mass destruction, machines that pollute the environment and so on. According to John Avery, what we choose to do with this technology is a matter of life and death.

Creation and use of nuclear weaponry during the Second World War is an example of how the advancement in science and technology proved to be extremely devastating and resulted in violence that persuaded the world to re-think over their strategies and actions. It was soon after Hiroshima and Nagasaki were bombarded with atomic fission bombs that the leaders of the world realized the great mistake that was committed. Scientists from the Manhattan Project, including Robert Oppenheimer understood that they had come up with a technology that was way too devastating to be handed over to humans. Later, the United States recognized its fault and provided Japan with a nuclear umbrella in order to make up for the loss. Albert Einstein wrote, in a telegram to leading Americans in May 1946: "The unleashed power of the atom has changed everything save our modes of thinking and we thus drift toward unparalleled catastrophe". In addition, Dr Pervez Hoodhboy, in his book entitled **Confronting the bomb** narrates his concerns about the advancement in technology that has made it possible for any physics student to create a nuclear explosive. Hence, it could be concluded that majority of the specialists in the

IS THE WORLD LESS VIOLENT IN MODERN TIMES?

field do not approve of this technology and are of the view that it was a mistake to come up with such a thing in the first place.

On the other hand, some advocates of developing nuclear weaponry argue that it is vital for peace-making purposes. Kenneth Waltz, in his book entitled **More May Be Better**, discusses how nuclear weapons serve has a mean of deterrence for peace-making. He narrates that in case of a world full of states possess nuclear weaponry there would be absolute peace since it would bring about an element of avoidance to use nuclear weapons. However, it is important to note that deterrence is a matter of chance and it relies on the assumption that a state possessing nuclear weaponry would not use it as it would be deterred by the other state's nuclear weaponry. In addition, this idea of deterrence does not look promising enough on states with political instability and religious or other influences. Furthermore, since there has been a great increase in non-state actors and terrorism on the bases of religion or otherwise, such weaponry can go into the hands of such non-state actors who would not be reluctant to use it for their cause.

None the less, science and technology also play a role in promoting and maintaining peace and stability at national and international levels. An example to this could be the use of advanced forensic science and other means of tracking down criminals which could not have been as easy before the advent of specific technologies. In addition, better communication methods have helped bridge gaps between people all around the globe that has enhanced tolerance and therefore contributed in bringing about peace. Furthermore, advancements in technology are also being used in foreign relations and economic co-relations in order to help in maintaining peace at a global level.

Therefore, it can be concluded that science and technology serve mankind in a way that no other field can as long as they are used for peaceful purposes and within the ethical boundaries. But the same aspect can result in the most devastating factors if misused.

IS THE WORLD LESS VIOLENT IN MODERN TIMES?

Do nationalism and the creation of states help in making the world less violent?

Due to social changes, advancements in technology and changes in mind sets; the tribal system which was practiced by our ancestors gradually changed into the nation-states we live in today. This change also affects the tendency of violence in today's world.

John Avery is of the view that nationalism and the concept of sovereignty is a threat to international peace. He argues that nationalism makes individuals and nations willing to go to all extents in order to benefit their state and sovereignty allows them to do so. In addition, sovereignty of a state allows it to do whatever it wishes to within the geographical boundaries of the state. This could result in chaos which would eventually spread to other states since the world is converting into a global village. An example of this could be how in some states militants are being produced to carry out particular purposes; these militants can easily be transferred or in some cases assigned to other states which could damage the other state in a number of ways. As a result of this nations fail to consider the effects their actions have to the World's community. Although, international laws and obligations such as the International Court of Justice have been established to minimize such effects, they have not proved to be effective enough to stop this phenomenon.

Steven Pinker is of the view that the pacification processes, which involve the transformation of non-state societies (tribes) into societies that form a state and are governed by a central government greatly decrease the rate and chances of violence. This is because establishment of a state would allow the government to practice and enforce law and order that would decrease the intensity and frequency of violence. Since creation of states results in an organized system which is run by rules and regulations, the justice system has

IS THE WORLD LESS VIOLENT IN MODERN TIMES?

become more easy and affective.

It can be observed that both Avery and Pinker made strong arguments regarding the effects of nationalism and state system on peace and stability, However, Avery is talking about peace at an international level while Pinker is dealing with national peace and stability.

Does abolition of punishments like death penalty decrease violence?

The introduction of human rights, laws regarding free trial and fair punishments have resulted in many nations abolishing death penalty and other closely related punishments. According to Pinker, this is a part of the Humanitarian Revolution that is a step towards a decrease in violence.

He believes that abolition of such punishments results in a higher value of life in general. Furthermore, he believes that doing so would provide law enforcement ageneses with fewer chances to carry out acts of violence and aggression. He believes that such punishments are not very helpful at persuading criminals to carry out acts like murder and against spreading terror.

On the other hand, some people are of the view that abolition of death penalties and severe punishments for severe acts of crime would persuade criminals and terrorists to carry out such activities since the fear of them being executed would be absent. In addition, it is argued that the abolishing of such punishments may prove to be helpful in developed countries with better economic and education conditions, however it would fail in promoting peace when it comes to underdeveloped countries.

IS THE WORLD LESS VIOLENT IN MODERN TIMES?

What is the contribution of education and economics towards a world with less violence?

According to Pinker, literacy is one of the reasons why the world is less violent in modern times. He is of the view that literacy makes individuals more rational and helps them to understand and appreciate differences among people. In addition, it broadens the mind to think out of the box and hence decreases the chances of someone getting involved in violence.

John Avery, on the other hand, takes this debate to a global level and illustrates the importance of education for peace. He argues that individuals and nations should be educated about global ethics and should be educated to be loyal to the human race. He calls it, the national anthem of humanity.

John Avery also highlights facts on the great increase in wealth and infrastructure being spent on war fare. According to Stockholm International Peace Research Institute, almost a trillion UD dollars are being spent on armaments each year. It is important to note that this figure only illustrates the recorded wealth spent for such purposes where some states have mechanisms to make sure that spending for such purposes is not recorded. In addition, according to Avery, 40 percent of all research funds around the globe are being used for armament and warfare related research. Furthermore, there is an export of 17 billion USD per year for armaments from the first world to the third world countries. It is important to note that third worlds countries face political unrest and are not capable enough to handle these armaments effectively.

Hence, it can be concluded that the nations of the world are spending way too much on making the world are less peaceful place and policies and regulations regarding this need to be revised and implemented upon strictly.

IS THE WORLD LESS VIOLENT IN MODERN TIMES?

How effective is the role of international peace-making systems?

It was after the Second World War and the use of atomic fission bombs that the nations of the world decided to establish the Disarmament and International Security Committee (First Committee of the United Nations). The aim of this committee and the initial aim of the United Nations as a whole was to make sure a war like the Second World War does not take place and that global peace is ensured.

However, while many people see the United Nations as an organization that has full control over how nations behave and the international system is run. The UN, is actually a body that does not have a power of its own. It is the nations of the world that provide the United Nations with funds and take oath to abide by the rules and regulations as set after discussion among nations and consciences. Therefore, the United Nations is not powerful enough to maintain peace and stability all over the world unless the interests of particular powerful nations is inclined to do so.

Conclusion:

In my opinion, the world still has to go a long way before it could be considered as a peaceful place. I believe that as far as international peace is concerned, there has been a shift in the type, location and tactics of war. Once wars were fought between nations with a sole purpose to conquer more territory whereas now there has been an increase in civil wars and acts like war on terror against non-state actors.

I believe that measures should be taken to make sure science and technology is used for peaceful purposes and that no such weaponry or technology should be created that is a blow to the human civilization. Although there are regulations regarding this but they need to be made more strict and

IS THE WORLD LESS VIOLENT IN MODERN TIMES?

measures need to be taken in order to depoliticize organizations such as the United nations. In addition, these organizations should be able to generate resources so that they do not rely on states to run.

There should also be more strict laws and regulations aimed to regulate the resources being used on warfare and countries that develop such weapons should be made accountable in true means. The United Nations does impose sanctions on such members but they are violated with the help of other nations who do this for personal interests.

In addition, the idea of educating for global citizenship is gaining popularity with an increase in exchange programs .etc. around the globe. But this needs to me greatly increased and implemented on a broader level. It should also include the training of foreign, military and political personnel to make sure a nation considers the consequences of its actions.

Works Cited

Avery, J. *Space Age Sciene and Stone Age Politics* .

Hoodboy, P. (2013). *Confronting the bomb.* Karachi: Oxford University Press.

Kelly, C. C. (2009). *The Manhattan Project.* New York: Black Dog & Leventhal Publishers.

Pinker, S. *The Better Angels of our Nature* .

Waltz, K. (1981). The Spread of Nuclear Weapons: More May Be Better. *Adelphi Papers Number 171* .

YOUR KNOWLEDGE HAS VALUE

- We will publish your bachelor's and master's thesis, essays and papers

- Your own eBook and book - sold worldwide in all relevant shops

- Earn money with each sale

Upload your text at www.GRIN.com
and publish for free